To Evang Ai...

God Bless You!

Rev. Dr. Edith P. Lagenby

Spiritual Gifts

DO YOU KNOW WHAT THEY ARE AND ARE YOU USING THEM??

Edith P. Lazenby

WESTBOW
PRESS®
A DIVISION OF THOMAS NELSON
& ZONDERVAN

WestBow Press books may be ordered through booksellers or by contacting:

WestBow Press
A Division of Thomas Nelson & Zondervan
1663 Liberty Drive
Bloomington, IN 47403
www.westbowpress.com
844-714-3454

Scripture taken from the King James Version of the Bible.

The Living Bible copyright © 1971 by Tyndale House Foundation. Used by permission of Tyndale House Publishers Inc., Carol Stream, Illinois 60188. All rights reserved. The Living Bible, TLB, and the The Living Bible logo are registered trademarks of Tyndale House Publishers.

ISBN: 978-1-6642-6374-1 (sc)
ISBN: 978-1-6642-6375-8 (hc)
ISBN: 978-1-6642-6373-4 (e)

Library of Congress Control Number: 2022907210

Print information available on the last page.

WestBow Press rev. date: 5/31/2022

CONTENTS

The Holy Spirit works beyond us with the power and understanding of God's Word. Rev. Dr. Edith Lazenby has carved out another gem for us to ponder. I highly recommend this book be available in every Christian library, It provides a true understanding of the Spirit of God our Counselor, Comforter, Giver of Spiritual Gifts, and Indwells those who accepts Jesus as Savior. Prepare to be motivated and elevated in the acts and works of the Holy Spirit.

--Evangelist Dr. Doris L. Billups, Pastor
Living In God's Holy Truth Ministries, Inc.

"Do not be taken back because of your lack of knowledge. Read on and be renewed by the knowledge exposed. You will come away from this with a desire to use the gifts you discover you have. I ask GOD on your behalf to increase your wisdom and understanding with this reading."

--Author Dr. Carolyn T. Holmes-Hood

I dedicate this book to my mother (Mrs. Marjorie Lazenby) who has gone home to be with the Lord. She had the gift of wisdom, knowledge, and faith.

This book is also dedicated to the Holy Spirit who gave me the understanding God has gifts for the body of Christ to use to defeat the enemy and give glory to God; and for the prompting of the Holy Spirit to write about spiritual gifts in belief that the body of Christ will stir up the gift/ or gifts within them to bring glory and honor to our Lord Jesus.

This book is also dedicated to each and every individual who may read it and discover the hidden gems stored within them, and to the unsaved who do not know the Lord that they will accept the Lord and discover the hidden gems stored within.

The body of Christ needs to know that once you put off the old Adamic nature (the old man), you are filled with God's Holy Spirit to do the work He has called you to do. You have been given a gift to help others realize that Jesus is real, He loves you, and God will be glorified through your obedience.

Where are the gifts? Why aren't they being used today? Why are only a few people operating in the gifts when the gifts are for everyone who are born again into the kingdom of God?

So what do you mean by "spiritual gift"? Great question. No one ever told me about a spiritual gift or that I have one. I have a natural gift that I was born with, so is that what you are talking about? No. That is a natural gift that you were blessed to have when your mother birthed you.

A spiritual gift comes from God when you are born again, and saved from your sins. Sin? I don't have any sin, so what are you talking about? Romans 3:10, 23 (KJV) states, "As it is written, There is none righteous, no, not one: For all have sinned, and come short of the glory of God."

Our first parents, Adam and Eve, caused sin to enter the world because they disobeyed God. That decision caused a spiritual separation between God and humankind. A price had to be paid to regain our spiritual connections to God.

Once this connection is made, we receive a gift, or gifts, from God. The first gift we should seek is the gift of the Holy Spirit. Evidence of this gift is the ability to speak in tongues as the Spirit gives utterance. When we acknowledge that gift, we need to move on and find out what other gifts God blessed us with. This might take some time, so in the meantime, become aligned with a Bible-believing and Bible-teaching church, and seek God to discover your gifts.

First Corinthians 12 lists the gifts of the Spirit. This

list is not exhaustive because other gifts are listed in Romans 12:6–8; Ephesians 4:11; and 1 Peter 4:8–11 (KJV). As you read throughout scripture you will notice the gifts of the Spirit did not just originate in the New Testament. In the Old Testament they were given by God to a particular person to accomplish a specific task God wanted accomplished.

God has other gifts for you, such as those found in Exodus 31:1–6 (KJV), where God gifted Bezaleel and Aholiab with the gift of wisdom, understanding, and knowledge in all manner of workmanship in gold, silver, and brass. Other Old Testament verses of spiritual gifts are listed in Exodus 28:3; Joshua 3:4–9; Micah 3:8; 1 Kings 3:8–9; 17:1–2 (KJV). Elisha stirred his gift with the help of a musician (2 Kings 3:15 KJV); Samson stirred his gift by shaking himself (Judges 16:20 KJV). Other examples of how people discovered the gifts within them can also be found in the Bible. What about you? Isn't it time you stirred up your gift?

Supporting Scriptures

Having then gifts differing according to the grace that is given to us, whether prophecy, let us prophesy according to the proportion of faith. (Romans 12:6 KJV)

Now concerning spiritual gifts, brethren, I would not have you ignorant. (1 Corinthians 12:1 KJV)

Ye know that ye were Gentiles, carried away unto these dumb idols, even as ye were led. Wherefore I give you to understand, that no man speaking by the Spirit of God called Jesus accursed: and that no man can say that Jesus is the Lord, but by the Holy Ghost. Now there are diversities of gifts, but the same Spirit. And there are differences of administration, but the same Lord. And there are diversities of operations, but it is the same God which worketh all in all. (1 Corinthians 12:2–9 KJV)

Neglect not the gift that is in thee, which was given thee by prophecy, with the laying on of the hands of the presbytery. (1 Timothy 4:14 KJV)

Wherefore I put thee in remembrance that thou stir up the gift of God, which is in thee by the putting on of my hands. (2 Timothy 1:6 KJV)

As every man hath received the gift, even so minister the same one to another, as good stewards of the manifold grace of God. (1 Peter 4:10 KJV)

CHAPTER 1

Understanding the Spiritual Gifts

We have experienced many revivals and crusades, such as the Azusa Street revival in California, the time of crusades with people such as Katherine Kuhlman, Oral Roberts, R. W. Shambach, Morris Cerullo, and evangelist Billy Graham. We've had some outstanding ministries such as those by A. A. Allen, Apostle Johnnie Washington, Auturo Skinner, and Benny Hinn. In all these revivals and services, we have seen people saved, delivered, healed, and set free from numerous conditions. But what we have not seen is the continuation of the gifts of the Spirit moving.

Where are they? Have they stopped now that we have entered the twenty-first century and the electronic age? Does a minister today still operate in the supernatural, or has God taken away the gifts of the Spirit from the body of Christ? I do not think so. Romans 11:29 (KJV) states, "For the gifts and calling of God are without repentance." The gifts of God are still in existence and operation, but they are not being used in the body of Christ today.

We are now living in the era called the electronic

age because we are so dependent on electronics in our daily lives. We have computers, cell phones, cell towers, electronic doorbells, smartphones, televisions that can monitor your every move, robots that help doctors perform operations, robots that can clean your floors and homes, drones that can take pictures and go where no one can go, and other electronic devices we do not know about. We can now carry electronic Bible versions (and some ungodly things) in our pockets or purses. We may have regulated God to second place, so to speak.

I realize people do not want to hear this because it is so easy to download a copy of one of the several versions of the Bible, and no one knows you are a Christian. Even little children know how to operate the computer and cell phone, and they are learning at an early age how to read. Children know how to download apps on their phones, but one essential app is missing—the Bible. They appear to be learning about everything except the Word of God on their electronic devices. If we have the app but do not use it, and if we do not read the Bible in any other form, there is no way we will know that God has gifts for his children.

All of us who have given our lives to Christ and accepted Jesus as our Lord and Savior have received gifts from God. You might ask, "What kind of gift have I received from God?" The gift of faith. It was from hearing and responding to the Word of God that faith arose in your heart, and you knew that Jesus was and is the Son of God, our Savior from sin. Ephesians 2:8–9 (KJV) states, "For by grace are ye saved through faith; and that not of yourselves: it is the gift of God: not of works, lest any man should boast."

Faith is one of the gifts listed in 1 Corinthians chapter 12. Many of us have often read 1 Corinthians chapter 12, but if you are like me, it really did not register that God has gifts to give his children for the perfecting of the church. Non-Christians have no interests in spiritual gifts or the Holy Spirit. But Christians should be hungering and thirsting after the things of God. As we look at the ministry of Christ while he was on earth, we notice everywhere he went he preached about the kingdom of heaven with signs and wonders following. Signs and wonders draw people to the place, or should I say to an atmosphere where God is moving. It's time we start fulfilling God's calls for our lives by studying his Word and seeking his face to see what gifts he has given us and what gifts may be operating in our lives.

Many people are ignorant to the fact that they have God-given gifts even though the Bible states, "I would not have you ignorant" (1 Corinthians 12:1b KJV). The reason could be because:

1. They were never told about spiritual gifts, so they are unaware these gifts exist.
2. They do not understand how to use the gifts.
3. They were afraid if they told anyone about their gifts that they would be made fun of.

4. There is jealousy in the body of Christ because someone has a particular gift and they do not.
5. Some leaders do not want their parishioners to know about these gifts, or use these gifts because of an ego problem.
6. Some leaders fear they might look bad because God does not use them in a particular gift.

So with this said, do spiritual gifts exist today? Yes they do. We read about them in books. But we must be careful what we read. A few biblical scholars and writers get it wrong. For example, John F. Walvoord stated in his book *The Holy Spirit* that these gifts as written in 1 Corinthians 12 ceased at the death of the apostles, which is untrue. Let me pause here and quote a few things Mr. Walvoord stated in his book. On the topic of the gift of discerning spirits, Mr. Walvoord writes,

> In connection with demon possession, as encountered particularly in heathen lands by missionaries, no doubt the same method of testing can be used. In any case, however, the gift of discerning spirits seems to be no longer bestowed. Christians are dependent now upon the written Word of God as illuminated by the Holy Spirit, and no one is

given authority to discern spirits apart from that belonging to all Christians alike.[1]

Under the gift of miracles, Mr. Walvoord states, "Gifts of miracles ceased at the end of the apostolic age."[2]

Under gift of prophecy, he writes,

While it may be freely admitted that men today possess the gift of teaching, the gift of exhortation, and the gift of evangelism, it is a safe conclusion that none possess the gift of prophecy.[3]

The gifts as found in 1 Corinthians 12:1–14 (KJV) are for the Christian believer today as they were when the Bible was written. They are very important today to draw the unsaved to Christ and to give hope to the Christian who does not know these gifts exist.

So once again, when you accept Jesus Christ as your Lord and Savior and are born again, you receive a spiritual gift, the gift of faith, and possibly baptism in the Holy Spirit evidenced by speaking in other tongues as the Spirit gives utterance. It is up to you to find out what other spiritual gift or gifts you have received. It is important that everyone

---

[1] Walvoord, John F., AM, ThD, *The Holy Spirit* (Grand Rapids, MI: Academie Books, Zondervan, 1958), p.188.

[2] Walvoord, p. 179.

[3] Walvoord, p. 178.

discovers what gifts they have been given by God. But how does a person find out what gift or gifts he or she has received from the Lord?

The heavenly gift given to us by the Holy Spirit is the gift of speaking in other languages, or what is known as speaking in tongues. Tongues allow the individual to speak in a heavenly language directly to the Father without the fear of the prayer being sabotaged by the enemy. An example of your prayer or the answer to your prayer being hindered is found in the book of Daniel. It took twenty-one days for Daniel to receive an answer to his prayer because it was held up by the prince of the kingdom of Persia, the enemy assigned to rule over that area.

> "Then said he unto me, Fear not, Daniel: for from the first day that thou didst set thine heart to understand, and to chasten thyself before thy God, thy words were heard, and I am come for thy words. But the prince of the kingdom of Persia withstood me one and twenty days; but, lo, Michael, one of the chief princes, came to help me; and I remained there with the kings of Persia. Now I am come to make thee understand what shall befall thy people in the latter days: for yet the vision is for many days" (Daniel 10:12–14 KJV).[4]

---

[4] *The Scofield Study Bible* (New York Oxford University Press, 1996), p. 916.

So how can you discover your gifts?

1. Seek the Lord through fasting and praying.
2. Make sure you are in a Bible-believing and Bible-teaching church.
3. Have someone mentor you.
4. Read the Word of God on your own.
5. Make time to spend in God's presence.
6. Ask the Lord to fill you with the Holy Spirit as the Word states.

Your gift must be cultivated, so you need to be in a church where gifts are being manifested. The gift is given to you by the Holy Spirit. Whatever the gift, its first purpose is to glorify the Lord, not yourself. We should not take credit for what the Lord has given us, whether it be speaking in tongues as the Spirit gives utterance, prophesying to someone, praying for the sick to be healed, or using administrative skills—which is the ability to put things in order and is sometimes referred to as the ability to govern—or any other gift you might have. So in essence, the gift you have received is something you were not able to do before.

We must remember that everyone who goes to the altar or say they are saved are not who they say they are. There are imposters, and we need to realize even with the spiritual gifts, there are imposters. We receive these gifts only through the Holy Spirit. I was surprised to learn there are schools that teach you how to speak in tongues. I personally do not believe in this because tongues are from God: "But ye shall receive power, after that the Holy Ghost is come upon you" (Acts 1:8a KJV);[5] "He that believeth on me, as the scripture hath said, out of his belly shall flow rivers of living waters"[6] (John 7:38 KJV).

Tongues come from your spirit man, not the fleshly soul man. So be aware there are counterfeit gifts given by Satan just as there are real spiritual gifts given by the Holy Spirit. Your spirit, your inner man, will bear witness whether someone else's spirit is real or not. So in essence 1 John 4:1b (KJV) states, "try the spirits whether they are of God."

Before we go in depth concerning the gifts of the Spirit, let us first look further at where and from whom these gifts come. They come through the Comforter, a.k.a. the Holy Ghost, a.k.a. the Holy Spirit. They are one and the same, but people address them differently.

Jesus told us in John 14:16–28 (KJV) that he had to go away. He could not remain on earth physically because after his work was complete, he had to return to his Father. When our work is complete, we also must return to our Creator God to give an account of our work here on earth. Jesus in his human form could only be in one place at a time, but the Comforter, the third person of the Godhead,

---

[5] *The Scofield Study Bible*, p. 1148.
[6] *The Scofield Study Bible*, p. 1125.

can be everywhere at once because the Comforter is a Spirit.

There is a difference between spiritual gifts as found in Corinthians and the fruit of the Spirit as found in the book of Galatians. Here are the nine fruit of the Spirit so you will see the difference between the two:

1. Love
2. Joy
3. Peace
4. Patience
5. Kindness
6. Goodness
7. Faithfulness
8. Gentleness
9. Temperance (self-control)

According to 1 Corinthians 12:1–11 (KJV) the gifts of the Spirit include the following:

1. The word of wisdom
2. The word of knowledge
3. Faith
4. Gifts of healing
5. Working of miracles
6. Prophecy
7. Discerning of spirits
8. Divers kinds of tongues
9. Interpretation of tongues

In Romans 12:6–8 (KJV) we find another listing of gifts, some of which have been referred to and some not. They are as follows:

1. Prophecy
2. Ministry
3. Teaching
4. Exhortation
5. Giving
6. Ruling
7. Mercy

Yes, some of these gifts are mentioned in 1 Corinthians, but no gift that we are blessed to have is more important than any other gift.

Additionally, in Ephesians chapter 4:8–12 (KJV), we find the fivefold ministry gifts:

1. Apostles
2. Prophets
3. Evangelists
4. Pastors
5. Teachers

for the perfecting (growth or growing into maturity) of the saints, for the work of the ministry, for the edifying of the body of Christ. (Ephesians 4:8–12 KJV)

Here, we have chosen leaders to help and teach the body of Christ. The spiritual gifts I am speaking about are found in 1 Corinthians chapter 12; and Romans chapter 12 are for the saints, the children of God, to help spread the gospel and reach people in areas pastors, evangelists, teachers, and so on are unable to reach or may not have the ability to perform, such as administration. Everyone does not have the know-how to keep things in order, file papers, type letters, and so on; the Lord has gifted individuals to perform these tasks. (See Exodus regarding God and the tabernacle.) God can take someone who has never read a note or played an instrument and place this gift in him or her once the individual accepts the Lord Jesus into his or her life.

But isn't a talent that a person is born with the same as a gift? No. I am glad you asked. A *talent* is an ability you are born with. An example could be your parents were musically inclined, and while the mother was carrying you, she played musical instruments or sang songs or maybe played in a band and constantly practiced her instrument. This may have been passed on to the baby, who later experienced a tendency to sing or play a musical instrument.

Or take, for example, a person just loves being around older people and helping them do things, while another doesn't. Then there is the person who love being around babies or young children, while another person will find they are unable to cope with children. These are talents. Gifting can be applied in this sense that God can enable a person who in the natural cannot stand to be around children become sensitive to the needs of children.

Let us look first at the Holy Spirit so we can get an understanding of who He is and why He is so important. The Holy Spirit is first mentioned in the book of Genesis where it states in chapter one verse two,

> "And the earth was without form, and void; and darkness was upon the deep. And the Spirit of God moved upon the face of the waters" (Genesis 1:2 KJV).[7]

Number one, we note that the Word *Spirit* starts with a capital "S," a noun–indicating a person, the third person of the triune God. Since many people do not understand when we use or say triune God, what I am talking about is God manifested in three distinct roles, but one person, God the Father, God the Son, and God the Holy Ghost. To better understand this let us take a piece of fruit, say an apple. Well, first of all we have the outer peeling; then we have the meat of what is found underneath the peeling; then we have the seeds, and all these components make up the apple, or any fruit for that matter. Then there is the human factor, mind, body, and spirit. So, in essence everything is triune.

Let us look at a few attributes of the Holy Spirit and why he is so important. The first thing Jesus told the

---

[7] *The Scofield Study Bible*, p. 3.

disciples was that he had to go away, but he would send us a Comforter, someone who would be here and everywhere at one time. After all, Jesus could only be in one place at a time in his human body. The Holy Spirit

1. convicts you of sin (John 16:8 KJV),
2. comforts you (Matthew 11:28 KJV),
3. draws you to Christ (Acts 2:41 KJV),
4. intercedes for you (Romans 8:26 KJV),
5. indwells you (Romans 8:9 KJV),
6. transforms you (Philippians 1:6 KJV),
7. preserves you (1 Peter 1:5 KJV),
8. leads you (Psalm 23:2 KJV), and
9. helps you pray (Romans 8:26 KJV).

It is the Holy Spirit who gives the gifts. "But ye shall receive power, after the Holy Ghost is come upon you" (Acts 1:8a KJV). He reveals deep things of God (1 Corinthians 2:9–10 KJV).

As stated previously, these are just a few of the attributes of the Holy Spirit. We can do nothing on our own without the leading of the Holy Spirit.

The Holy Spirit is omnipotent, all powerful (Colossians 1:15–20 KJV; Matthew 19:26 KJV). The Holy Spirit possesses strength, power, and has great control or authority. He has unlimited universal power and controls nature and all that is therein.

The Holy Spirit is omnipresent; he is present

everywhere because the Holy Spirit is a Spirit, the Spirit of God (Deuteronomy 4:29 KJV). Jesus in his human form could only be in one place at a time (Matthew 28:20 KJV). The psalmist, David, asked, "Where can I go from your presence" (Psalm 139:7–12 KJV).

The Holy Spirit is omniscience, all knowing. He knows all things. He has infinite awareness, understanding, and insight (Luke 16:15 KJV; Acts 15:18 KJV).

The Holy Spirit indwells you: "And I will put my spirit within you, and cause you to walk in my statues, and ye shall keep my judgments, and do them" (Ezekiel 36:27 KJV). But in 2 Timothy 1:14 (KJV), we find these words: "That good thing which was committed unto thee keep by the Holy Ghost which dwelleth in us."

Once the old man of sin is put off, we who are born anew can invite the new man—the Holy Spirit—to come and dwell within us and lead us. As Christians we want the Holy Spirit to dwell within us because then we know he abides within us (Romans 8:9 KJV).

The Holy Spirit regenerates us, which means being born again, turning from our old man and the putting on our new man, the Holy Spirit. First Corinthians 15:17; John 1:13; 3:3–7; Romans 6:13 KJV are examples.

The Holy Spirit is instrumental in everything. It is through the movement of the Holy Spirit, working in conjunction with the Father and Son, that spiritual gifts are manifested to believers. Now let us look at the spiritual gifts in more depth.

CHAPTER 1
Questions

1. Have the gifts of the spirit ceased operation today? If so, why? If not, why not?

_____

_____

_____

_____

2. Name some of the gifts listed in 1 Corinthians:12.

_____

_____

_____

_____

3. List some of the gifts in Romans 12:6–8 KJV.

_____

_____

_____

_____

4. List some of the gifts in Ephesians 4:8–12 KJV.

_____

_____

_____

_____

5. Who is the Comforter?

_____

_____

6. Name a few things the Comforter does for you.

_____

_____

_____

_____

7. What is the difference between a talent and a gift?

_____

_____

_____

_____

CHAPTER 2

The Fivefold Ministry Gifts (Ephesians 4:11–12 KJV)

As mentioned previously, when we are born, God gives us a natural talent. Some can sing like a bird, and others can play instruments with or without taking lessons. Some people are natural-born speakers, while some are able to grasp and understand a subject such as physics with ease. Some people are natural leaders, while others need practice to be good leaders. These are just a few of the talents we can be born with. We just need to discover what that talent is.

As in the natural, so in the spiritual. When people are born again, when they accept Jesus into their lives, God gives each of them at least one gift. It is left to us to find out what that gift is. Your spiritual man, who was lying dormant in your belly, came alive, and you put on the new man of Christ Jesus. For the Word states in John 7:37–38 (KJV), "If any man thirst, let him come unto me, and drink. He that believeth on me, as the scripture hath said, out of his belly shall flow rivers of living water." John 3:16 (KJV) says, "You must be born again." What does this mean because here I am, walking about, eating, sleeping, and doing ordinary everyday things? I am alive. Your soul man is alive, but your spirit man is dead. He needs to be resurrected, and the only way that can happen is to be born again from above, not from below.

A spiritual gift is different from a natural talent. According to God, you can have more than one gift because it comes from God and not a human. A spiritual gift is a God-given special ability given to every believer at conversion, or the moment you acknowledge the Lord Jesus as your Savior. The Holy Spirit gives you your gifts to share his love, and compassion and to strengthen the body of Christ. Your gift is to be used to serve the body of Christ and to glorify God.

Unfortunately, most of these God-given gifts are rarely used in most church settings because people are not taught about the gifts. And should they inquire about them, the most frequent answer is often that they are not for today, that they died with the apostles, or I don't know. So the gifts that God has given us lie dormant because either the leader doesn't know the gifts exist, knows the gifts exists but doesn't want to share the information with you, or we as a body refuse to accept the gifts God has to offer. Hosea 4:6 (KJV) states, "my people are destroyed for lack of knowledge: because thou hast rejected knowledge, I will also reject thee."

We read the Word of God, but we do not become

inquisitive enough to find out for ourselves what the Word of God means. The Holy Spirit, or Comforter, lies waiting to be activated in the saved individual. But most of us are oblivious to the fact that the Holy Spirit even exists within us. Therefore, in most churches, we find spirit-filled individuals just sitting in the pew doing nothing, believing that the gifts and calling are only for the pastor or leader. But we find these words in Mark 16:17–18 (KJV):

> And these signs shall follow them that believe; in my name shall they cast out devils; they shall speak with new tongues; they shall take up serpents; and if they drink any deadly thing, it shall not hurt them; they shall lay hands on the sick, and they shall recover.

This scripture tells us if you have been born again, believe in Jesus, you should be doing the same things Jesus did because the power and gifts have been given to you.

When you do see individuals working in the local church, most are not taking full advantage of their spiritual gifts. This could be why some people have no joy in these positions; they are serving in the wrong office. It is important that we have a proper understanding of these spiritual gifts. We need to unfold what the gifts are and learn a little about each one.

So how do you know what gift, or gifts, you have of the Spirit? Why should someone be concerned about having a spiritual gift? The gifts are given by the Spirit of God, whereby he can be glorified, and the believer as well as the unbeliever will come to an understanding that God exists.

When you think of spiritual gifts, we automatically think of Ephesians 4:11 KJV, which tells of the fivefold ministry gifts—apostles, prophets, evangelists, pastors, and teachers. The purpose of the fivefold ministry gifts, as stated in Ephesians 4:11–16 KJV, is to help the ministry flow together in the body with love. Another purpose of the fivefold ministry gifts is to train other believers to discover and use the gifts given to them by the Holy Spirit. Let's take a brief look at each of the fivefold ministry gifts.

The Apostle: Ephesians 4:11; 1 Corinthians 12:28 KJV. Many today have stated that the office of the apostle no longer exists. According to those with that opinion, it was only initiated by Jesus for the twelve apostles he chose—Matthew; Mark; Luke; John; Peter; James; Philip; Bartholomew; Thomas; Thaddaeus; Simeon the Zealot; and Judas Iscariot, who was replaced by Matthias and then by Paul. What does the word "apostle" mean? It means "one who is sent" or "messenger." *Unger's Bible Dictionary* explains it this way: "one sent with a special message or commission."[8] Their primary role is to help raise up churches to preach the gospel of Jesus Christ.

The primary job Jesus's apostles had after his death was to go and spread the gospel of Jesus Christ, but they chose to stay in Jerusalem. Only through persecution that arose

---

[8] Merrill F. Unger, *Unger's Bible Dictionary* (Chicago: Moody Press, 1987), p. 72.

did the apostles go to various countries and surrounding areas to spread the gospel (Acts 8:1–8 KJV).

Additionally, we see the role of an apostle as one who is commissioned and sent by a church or a church planter to preach the gospel. And through them, new communities and believers are established, commissioned, and sent out by a church (Matthew 10:2; Acts 5:12; 1 Corinthians 12:28; Hebrews 3:1–2 KJV).

Prophet: Acts 11:27–28; Romans 12:6; 1 Corinthians 12:10, 28, 14:3; Ephesians 4:11 KJV. According to *Unger's Bible Dictionary,* "a prophet or prophetess is a person, or persons who are divinely inspired to communicate God's will to his people and to disclose the future to them."[9] In addition, a prophet is regarded as being in contact with a divine being and who speaks on his or her behalf. He or she delivers messages or teachings from the Lord to other people.

The first mention of a prophet or prophetess is mentioned in the Old Testament. God used both men and women in the office of prophet or prophetess. Miriam is the first woman spoken of as a prophetess (Exodus 15:20 KJV) followed by Deborah (Judges 4:4 KJV). The first male prophet spoken of was Moses.

Prophets have been used through the ages to speak to heads of nations with warnings to turn from their wicked ways back to the Lord. Additionally, prophets and

---

[9] Unger, p. 890.

prophetess are also used by God in churches and other gatherings to warn people, to build up lives, and to comfort others. The main function of the prophet is to exhort, comfort, and encourage people (1 Corinthians 14:1, 31; 12:29; Acts 21:8–11 KJV).

Evangelist: Ephesians 4:11; John 1:45–46; Acts 21:8–9 KJV. The role of the evangelist is to preach and teach the good news, which is the Word of God. Evangelists do not have churches of their own. They travel from place to place, preaching the gospel to draw souls to Jesus Christ. The message they preach should clearly describe who Jesus is so people's faith can be uplifted.

While preaching or teaching, it is imperative that the evangelist draw people to Jesus, not to themselves. As in any occupation the evangelist will have some bad experiences, but this should not stop the evangelist from preaching the gospel. No matter what, the evangelist must make sure all the attention goes to Christ. The importance of the cross and the blood of Jesus must be preached. They take precedence over human-made doctrines and laws.

Pastor: Ephesians 4:11; John 10:1–18; 1 Peter 5:4 KJV. A pastor is an individual called by God to shepherd a flock—a congregation of people—teaching, sharing the Word of God, and leading them in the right direction. The pastor should be the one to preach or teach on Sunday mornings and afternoons. He should be available to visit and pray for the sick, counsel people, comfort people in their times of need, and help take care of the needs of the people. The pastor needs to be well versed and have a good understanding of the scriptures.

The pastor is the servant of the people. The pastor also performs administrative duties, such as ensuring there is a music ministry in place, a youth ministry for the youth, and competent Sunday school teachers. The pastor must also be able to perform weddings, funerals, and conduct business meetings (1 Peter 5:4 KJV; John 10:1–18 KJV).

Teacher: Ephesians 4:11 KJV. The teacher should adhere to 2 Timothy 2:15 (KJV): "study to shew thyself approved unto God, a workman that needeth not to be ashamed, rightly dividing the word of truth."

The teacher opens the understanding of the Word of God by comparing precept upon precept, line upon line. Both pastors and teachers can be interchangeable within the body of Christ. If a pastor is not available, then the teacher should be able to preach the Word and explain the scriptures to the congregation, and vice versa.

Teachers are able to pass on their knowledge to others. Not only in a Christian setting, but also in a grade school, high school, or any other institution of learning. But to get the basic understanding of the Bible, it is important to attend a church with a knowledgeable person teaching God's Word (1 Corinthians 12:28; Romans 12:7; Hebrews 5:12 KJV).

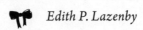

CHAPTER 2
Questions

1. Do you know the difference between a talent and a spiritual gift? Explain the difference.

   _____

   _____

   _____

   _____

2. What is the best way to find out what your spiritual gift is?

   _____

   _____

   _____

   _____

3. What is the purpose of a spiritual gift?

   _____

   _____

   _____

   _____

4. Who can and cannot have a spiritual gift? In other words, can everyone have a spiritual gift?

_____

_____

_____

_____

5. What are the fivefold ministry gifts as described in Ephesians 4:11 (KJV). Explain each one.

_____

_____

_____

_____

6. What scripture tells you," and these signs shall follow them that believe"?

_____

_____

_____

_____

CHAPTER 3

The Spiritual Gifts: The Knowing Gifts

The Spirit's gifts have been divided into three categories to make it easier to distinguish and understand:

The revelation spiritual gifts, or the knowing gifts:

- The word of wisdom
- The word of knowledge
- The gift of discerning of spirits or distinguishing of spirits

The spiritual gifts of utterance, or gifts that say something:

- The gift of prophecy
- The gift of diverse tongues
- The gift of interpretation of tongues

The power gifts, or gifts that do something:

- The gift of faith
- The gift of miracles
- The gift of healing

If we continue reading 1 Corinthians 12:1–28 KJV, there are other gifts that are rarely mentioned. These gifts are administration, discernment, exhortation (also known as encouragement), evangelism, faith, giving, helps, hospitality, knowledge, leadership, mercy, preaching, service, pasturing (a.k.a. shepherding), teaching, and wisdom.

Before we look at the meaning of the gifts, let's first define the word "supernatural," which is mentioned numerous times. "Supernatural—1. existing or occurring outside the normal experience or knowledge of man; caused by other than the known forces of nature. 2. attributed to hypothetical forces beyond nature; miraculous; divine."[10] Since 1828, the *Merriam-Webster Dictionary* has described "supernatural" as "1. Of or relating to an order of existence beyond the visible observable universe especially: of or relating to God or a god, demigod, spirit, or devil. 2. Departing from what is usual or normal especially so as to appear to transcend the laws of nature. 3. Attributed to an invisible agent (such as a ghost or spirit)."[11]

---

[10] *College Edition Webster's New World Dictionary of the American Language* (Cleveland: The World Publishing Company, 1966, p. 1464).

[11] Merriam-Webster.com/dictionary/supernatural.

Let us look at the meaning of some of these gifts so we can get an understanding of their operation.

The Word of Wisdom: Acts 11:28 (KJV). This gift is the supernatural ability of the Holy Spirit to relay God's knowledge of His plan and purpose that will be fulfilled in the future for a person, place, or thing. It is also revealed to resolve a problem for protection and to escape from something. The word of wisdom can be revealed within a believer's spirit as an intuition, a dream, or a vision, or by the written Word of God. It can be confirmed through a minister, such as a prophet, or through any other spirit-filled believer. An example of how wisdom was used in the Old Testament occurred when King Solomon used wisdom when he had to decide whose child had died and whose child was alive (1 Kings 3:12 KJV). His actions brought out the truth about the child's real mother. Gifts of wisdom and knowledge were and are given to people to communicate God's truth.

In some instances, we find the word of wisdom and the word of knowledge working in conjunction with each other through the unction of the Holy Spirit. An example of this occurred when the Holy Spirit revealed to Ananias God's plan and purpose for Saul (Acts 9:10–17 KJV). Another example of the word of wisdom is when Agabus the prophet took the girdle that belonged to Paul and spoke what the Holy Ghost told him to say, which was that the Jews at Jerusalem would bind the man who "owneth this girdle, and shall deliver him into the hands of the Gentiles"

(Acts 21:10, 11 KJV). The Bible states in Psalm 111:10 (KJV),

> The fear of the Lord is the beginning of wisdom: all who follow his precepts have good understanding.

The Word of Knowledge: 1 Corinthians 12:10 (KJV). Once again, the Holy Spirit supernaturally relays God's knowledge concerning certain facts or details of the past or present state or activities of a person, place, or thing the ministering individual knows nothing about. This can be revealed in the human spirit of the believer intuitively, in dreams or visions, by a still small voice of God, or by an empathetic feeling for the moment within a minister of healing of someone else's pain. This indicates that God is healing the hurting person, *not* the minister.

Some may mistakenly believe that the word of knowledge might be intellectual knowledge, something learned by going to school or reading a book about a subject. No, the word of knowledge is a supernatural impartation gift given to a spirit-filled person through the Holy Spirit. A few examples in the Bible include:

1. Hezekiah, who was sick unto death, prayed. God heard his prayer and added fifteen years to his life (2 Kings 20:6 KJV).

2. John, when on the isle of Patmos, God supernaturally revealed to him about things to come (Revelation 1:10–20 KJV).

3. Ananias had a vision from the Lord to go to a place and lay hands on Saul that he might receive his sight (Acts 9:11–12 KJV).

4. Peter went on a rooftop to pray and fell into a trance that was later explained to him meant not to call unclean things God called cleaned (Acts 10:9–13 KJV). God was opening a door to include Gentiles into the kingdom of God.

It is God, not a human, who gives you supernatural knowledge. This gift can be exercised in a prayer group, church setting, hospital, or nursing home. Wherever God may send you to minister to others.

The Gift of Discerning of Spirits or the Distinguishing of Spirits: Matthew 16:21–23; Acts 5:1–11; 16:16–18; 1 Corinthians 12:10 KJV. This important gift refers to the Holy Spirit's supernatural ability to reveal to a believer spirits in the spirit realm only. The believer is able to perceive, sense, or actually see in the spirit demonic activity and motives, discern the voice and presence of Satan, perceive and see angelic activity and motives, and see Jesus and sense his presence. As well as perceive something done by a human error out of ignorance and not by a demon spirit or an evil motive. This gift can be revealed in the spirit of a believer or in a dream or vision (when half-sleep, or in waking state called open vision). It can be determined through hearing demons, angels, Jesus's voice, Satan's voice, the singing voices of angels, trumpets in heaven, or heavenly music.

To break it down, discernment is the ability to recognize whether or not something or someone is truly from God or in accordance with righteousness. Just because something looks or seems right doesn't mean it's right because the adversary is a master of deception. The Holy Spirit gives us the gift of discernment to enable Christians to recognize and distinguish between what is of God, Satan, the world, and our flesh. According to Hebrews 5:13–14 KJV, this gift, which is truly needed today, helps Christians in times of danger and keeps them from being led astray by false doctrine. Every believer, whether a newborn babe in Christ or a seasoned saint, should ask the Lord for the gift of discernment, so we won't be caught unaware or off guard.

Does everyone have the gift of discernment of spirits? Yes and no. No, everyone can and should be able to determine what is right and what is wrong, but this is not always the case. Knowledge of the scriptures will help an individual determine what is right and what is wrong. The person who God, through the Holy Spirit, has presented the gift of discerning spirits has the ability to distinguish between the truth of the Word and the deceptive doctrines propagated by demons. An example of the gift in operation can be found in Acts 5:1–11 KJV, when Ananias and Sapphira conspired to lie to the Holy Ghost.

So everyone does not have the gift of discerning of spirits. This is one gift we should pray to receive because what we think is of the devil is often really of the flesh. We need to discern whether things are of God, our flesh, or of the devil.

In these three spiritual gifts, sometimes called the knowing gifts, you see the word of wisdom, the word of knowledge, and the distinguishing of spirits working in conjunction with each other. We must remember that all these manifestations come from the Lord.

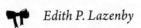

CHAPTER 3
Questions

1. What is meant by knowing gifts?

    _____

    _____

    _____

    _____

2. What are the knowing gifts?

    _____

    _____

    _____

    _____

3. Which gift is used in conjunction with the others?

    _____

    _____

    _____

    _____

4. Is discerning of spirit in operation today in the believer? If so, why? If not, why not?

    _____

    _____

    _____

    _____

5. List two times the word of wisdom was used in the Old Testament.

_____

_____

_____

6. What are some ways the word of wisdom was used in the Old Testament?

_____

_____

_____

_____

7. Name a few ways the word of knowledge was received by individuals.

_____

_____

_____

_____

CHAPTER 4

Gifts of Utterance: Gifts That Say Something

The Gift of Prophecy: 1 Corinthians 12:10; 14:3 KJV. "Prophecy means 1. Prediction of the future under the influence of divine guidance, act or practice of a prophet. 2. Any prediction. 3. something prophesied or predicted; specifically, the utterance or utterances of a prophet."[12] It is the supernatural ability of the Holy Spirit dwelling within a believer to edify, comfort, and exhort a person or the body of Christ. Proclaimed prophecy should never confuse, frighten, or discourage a person or the recipient. Rather, it should build spiritually, build self-esteem, comfort, and stir the recipient back on to the path of righteousness. This gift builds up and encourages us. It brings life and vision and light, not doom and gloom and death.

    The Gift of Diverse Tongues: 1 Corinthians 12:10; 14:1–14, 22; Acts 2:1–13; 10:44–47; 11:15–18 KJV. Again, we see the supernatural gift of the Holy Spirit being able to

---

[12] *College Edition Webster's New World Dictionary of the American Language,* p. 1168.

speak in various languages of different nationalities, or an angelic language not learned. Only God is able to use an individual to speak in a language unknown to him to give a message of edification, exhortation, or comfort, to a person, congregation, or group of people in their native tongues. For the message in tongues to be understood, the gift of interpretation must follow either through another spirit-filled believer who received the interpretation from God, or through the believer who spoke in tongues.

This gift is different from the devotional tongue every believer received when baptized with the Holy Spirit. This type of speaking in tongues is when the Holy Spirit prays through the spirit of the believer to God only, and not to people. The believer's understanding of the prayer tongue is unfruitful; however, the believer can ask the Holy Spirit for the interpretation. This gift cannot be learned or studied.

Of all the spiritual gifts, the hardest one to understand and receive is the gift of tongues as the Spirit gives utterance. I'm not saying that because you don't speak in tongues or another language as the Spirit gives you utterance you don't have the indwelling of the Holy Spirit. What I am saying is that this particular gift is given to the individual once they accept Christ. It's up to you, through faith, to seek the Lord and to stir up this gift that has been given you. Acts 2:38–39 (KJV) states,

Then Peter said, unto them, repent, and be baptized everyone of you in the name of Jesus Christ for the remission of sins, and ye shall receive the gift of the Holy Ghost. For the promise is unto you, and to your children, and to all that are afar off, even as many as the Lord our God shall call.

Gift of Interpretation: 1 Corinthians 14:27–28; Acts 2:1–13 KJV. This gift operates in conjunction with the gift of diverse tongues. The Holy Spirit interprets through the believer the meaning of what was said in diverse tongues so that the person, or the body of Christ in a church congregation, can be edified. The message that is understood is a form of prophecy because it edified, comforted, or exhorted the people. The interpretation can be revealed to and spoken by any believer to whom the Holy Spirit has revealed the interpretation. Or it can be revealed by the same believer through which the message in tongues was spoken.

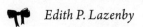

CHAPTER 4
Questions

1. What are the three components of prophecy?

   _____

   _____

   _____

2. Does everyone have the gift of diverse tongues?

   _____

   _____

   _____

   _____

3. What does having diverse tongues mean?

   _____

   _____

   _____

   _____

4. If a person prophesizes in an unknown tongue, can that same person interpret the tongue or message? Yes or no? Explain.

   _____

   _____

   _____

   _____

5. Can everyone speak in an unknown tongue?

_____

_____

_____

6. Who gives you the ability to speak in an unknown language?

_____

_____

_____

_____

7. Should prophecy frighten someone? If not, why not?

_____

_____

_____

_____

8. What three things is prophecy noted to do for someone?

_____

_____

_____

CHAPTER 5

The Power Gifts:
Gifts That Do Something

The Gift of Faith: 1 Corinthians 12:9 KJV. This gift is a supernatural manifestation of God's faith imparted to the believer to help him or her expect the impossible of what God is going to do and what will come to pass. This God kind of faith is not the same as human faith and saving faith, although in salvation, faith was given by God by the hearing of his Word. The gift of faith, however, is given by the Holy Spirit according to his will that the believer have faith that the impossible will happen.

When the Spirit of God endows someone with the gift of faith the intent is for that person to have extraordinary confidence in God's promises, power, and presence. The person who exercises the gift of faith has unshakable faith in God, his Word, and his promises. The best examples of people exercising this type of faith can be found in Hebrews chapter 11, which is sometimes called the "Hall of Faith" because it took divine faith to believe God when he spoke to these people. People with this gift can help others develop and exhibit a confidence in God which they did not previously have.

This gift, which is manifested by the Holy Spirit, enables someone to receive a miracle beyond the capacity of ordinary faith. If you remember, the three Hebrew boys exercised the gift of faith when they refused to bow down and worship the golden idol. It took faith in God that he would protect them (Daniel 3:19–26 KJV). Another example is when Daniel he was thrown in the lion's den. He exercised faith that the God he prayed to three times a day would deliver him, and he did (Daniel 6:22 KJV). Additionally, Elijah exercised faith when the raven, which was considered unclean, brought him food to eat twice a day during a famine in the land (1 Kings 17:3–6 KJV). These examples took the intervention of God's supernatural power for the faith of these people to be activated.

It was no ordinary faith. It was supernatural faith, unwavering faith, believing something extraordinary would occur through the divine intervention of God. "The gift of faith brings an inward calm within the spirit of those through whom this gift is manifested."[13]

The Gift of Miracles: 1 Corinthians 12:28, 10; Acts 19:11–12 KJV. This is the supernatural ability of the Holy Spirit or God to intervene in the course of nature for a moment, or within a given time, to cast out a demon,

---

[13] Kenneth E. Hagin, *The Holy Spirit and His Gifts Study Course* (Tulsa, OK: Faith Library Publication, 1991), p. 122.

replace a body part, open up the Red Sea, raise the dead, protect a person in a tragic accident, missing an accident involving a believer or person by a split second. The gift of faith often operates along with this gift because it allows the believer to expect the seemingly impossible miracle without doubt so that the Holy Spirit can manifest.

One of the greatest miracles is when a person accepts Jesus Christ as his or her Lord and Savior. The reason I say this is because all the forces of hell try to stop humankind from realizing that Jesus is the Savior, sent by God to redeem humankind from their sins. Such a supernatural miracle is when God parted the Red Sea and the children of Israel walked through on dry, not muddy, ground (Exodus 14:16–28 KJV). Another example of a miracle occurred when the head of an ax fell into the water, and when Elisha threw in a stick, the ax-head floated to the top (2 Kings 6:6 KJV). Another example of a miracle is when Jesus had the servants fill the pots with water, and by the spoken word, the water was turned into wine (John 2:7–11 KJV).

When Jesus fed the five thousand people with a little boy's lunch of two fishes and five loaves of bread (John 6:5–14 KJV), that was a miracle. And another example of a miracle was when the sun went back five degrees (Isaiah 38:1–8 KJV). To summarize, miracles are creative acts that go against the laws of nature.

The Gift of Healing: 1 Corinthians 12:7–9; Acts 3:6–8; 5:15–16; 9:32–41 KJV. The gift of healing is the supernatural ability of the Holy Spirit imparted within a believer by the Holy Spirit himself. This gives the believer an inward direction when his or her hands are laid on the sick recipient, or the recipient is healed without the laying of hands on him or her. This gift can be given by way of direction to heal in a dream or vision, by perception in a waking state, or by speaking a creative word as the Holy Spirit reveals a thought of what to say.

Not everyone is gifted with the gift of healing. However, some people with this gift are gifted to heal certain types of ailments through the moving of the Holy Spirit. Some have been endowed with the healing of people with cancer or the opening of deaf ears. Some have been gifted with the ability of laying hands on people with cancer and/or diabetes, and those people are healed. Everyone can lay hands on individuals and pray for them, but that doesn't mean they have the gift of healing.

It is important to know what area you are gifted in, or when the Holy Spirit wants to use you in a special way. We must remember it is not us who are doing the healing. It is the Holy Spirit moving through us to do the will of the Lord.

CHAPTER 5
Questions

1. What is the difference between the gift of faith and faith?

    _____

    _____

    _____

    _____

    _____

2. Does everyone have the gift of faith? If yes, why? If no, why not?

    _____

    _____

    _____

    _____

3. Would you consider the Israelites crossing the Red Sea a miracle or a natural phenomenon? Why?

    _____

    _____

    _____

    _____

4. What has occurred in your life that you would describe as a miracle?

_____

_____

_____

_____

5. Does God still heal today?

_____

_____

_____

_____

6. Are you able to heal someone without the Holy Spirit? If yes, why? If no, why not?

_____

_____

_____

_____

CHAPTER 6

Other Spiritual Gifts

Administration: Romans 12:8; 1 Corinthians 13:8; 12:8 KJV. This is also known as governments in the Bible. Someone with this gift has the ability to formulate and give directions, organize, make decisions on behalf of others, and carry out plans to fulfill a purpose. They should be able to delegate tasks to others, which makes it possible to accomplish more for the kingdom of God. One of the functions of administration is to train other believers for leadership positions in the church. An example of someone in a leadership position is Moses:

> And it came to pass on the morrow, that Moses sat to judge the people: and the people stood by Moses from the morning unto the evening. (Exodus 18:13 KJV)

Also,

> And when they had ordained them elders in every church, and had prayed with fasting,

they commended them to the Lord, on whom they believed. (Acts 14:23 KJV)

Exhortation: Romans 12:8; Acts 11:23–24; 14:21–22; 15:32 KJV. The gift of exhortation moves the believer to minister words of encouragement, consolation, comfort, and motivation from God's Word to help others complete their tasks and be all God wants them to be. The Spirit of God gives this gift to people in the church to strengthen and encourage them, especially those who are wavering in their faith. The goal of the encourager is to see everyone in the church continually build up the body of Christ and glorify God.

An example of exhortation can be found in the following scriptures, when God speaks to Joshua after Moses died:

> Moses my servant is dead: now therefore arise, go over this Jordan, thou, and all this people, unto the land which I do give to them, even to the children of Israel. (Joshua 1:2 KJV).

And,

> And when they preached the gospel to that city, and had taught many, they returned again to Lystra, and to Iconium, and Antioch, Confirming the souls of the disciples, and exhorting them to continue in the faith, and that we must through much tribulation

enter into the kingdom of God. (Acts 14:21–22 KJV)

Evangelism: Ephesians 4:11 KJV. This is the gift that enables believers to reach nonbelievers with the good news of salvation in such a way they become believers, are baptized, and become active members in the body of Christ. The evangelist is burdened in his or her heart for the lost and will go out of the way to share the truth with all types of people. Because of this, they are able to draw more people to Christ with the gospel of salvation through Jesus Christ.

Scripture specifically speaks of Philip being an evangelist (Acts 2:18 KJV). Everyone should be an evangelist because we are responsible for telling others about salvation through Jesus Christ. An example of a gospel message an evangelist could bring is this:

> Therefore let all the house of Israel know assuredly, that God hath made that same Jesus, whom ye have crucified, both Lord and Christ. Now when they heard this, they were pricked in their heart, and said unto Peter and to the rest of the apostles, Men and brethren, what shall we do? (Acts 2:36–37 KJV)

Faith: 1 Corinthians 12:8–10 KJV. The gift of faith gives the believer the eyes to see the Spirit at work. And when challenged by ideas most see as impossible, the gift of faith gives the believer the ability to trust the Spirit's lead without indication of where it will go. Having faith gives the believer the realization that he or she has no control over matters, and what will be, will be. They rely on God to intervene in situations they have no control over.

An example of faith in action is when Peter told the lame man to walk: "Then Peter said, silver and gold have I none; but such as I have give I thee: in the name of Jesus Christ of Nazareth rise up and walk" (Acts 3:6 KJV).

In Acts 27:22–24 (KJV) Paul boldly declares during a shipwreck,

> And now I exhort you to be of good cheer: for there shall be no loss of any man's life among you, but of the ship. For there stood by me this night the angel of God, whose I am, and whom I serve, saying, Fear not, Paul; thou must be brought before Caesar: and, lo, God hath give thee all them that sail with thee.

Giving: Romans 12:8; 2 Corinthians 9:6–8; Malachi 3:8 KJV. The gift of giving enables a believer to recognize God's blessings and to respond to those blessings by generously and sacrificially giving of one's resources, time, talent, and treasure. This type of gift should not come with any strings attached. It is done from the heart without the need for efforts to be recognized, such as the Pharisees did.

Another example of giving is when the children of Israel

asked for donations of silver and gold to help build the tabernacle. The people were to give willingly and their donation would be received (Exodus 25:2 KJV). Whatever you give to God should be done willingly and from your heart and in love (Luke 6:28 KJV). An example of giving can be found in 2 Corinthians 9:7 (KJV): "Every man according as he purposeth in his heart, so let him give not grudgingly, or of necessity for God loveth a cheerful giver."

Another example is found in Luke 6:38 (KJV):

> Give, and it shall be given unto you, good measure, pressed down, and shaken together, and running over, shall men give into your bosom. For with the same measure that ye mete withal it shall be measured to you again.

Helps: 1 Corinthians 12:28; Romans 16:1–2 KJV. To receive the God-given ability to help is to serve and strengthen the body of Christ by rejoicing in the success of others, serving behind the scenes, and enjoying what others are doing, and looking for ways to assist others (1 Corinthians 12:28 KJV). A perfect example of the gift of helps is found in the story of Moses. When the Israelites were fighting, as he held his arms up, they would be winning. But when he lowered his arms, they would lose. So Hur and Aaron held up Moses's arms (Exodus 17:9–12 KJV).

Another instance of the gift of helps can be found in

Romans 16:3–4 (KJV). Pricilla and Aquila went out of their way to help Paul and risked their lives in doing so. They did not have to do it, but they did.

Examples of someone needing help can be found in the following:

> But Martha was cumbered about much serving and came to him, and said, Lord dost thou not care that my sister hath left me to serve alone? bid her therefore that she help me. (Luke 10:40 KJV)

And,

> Likewise the Spirit also helpeth our infirmities for we know not what we should pray for as we ought: but the Spirit itself maketh intercession for us with groanings which cannot be uttered. (Romans 8:26 KJV)

Hospitality: Matthew 25:35, 40; Romans 12:9, 13; 1 Timothy 3:2; 1 Peter 4:9–10 KJV. This gift enables a believer to joyfully welcome and receive guests and those in need of food and lodging. People with the gift of hospitality are known for making those around them feel valued, cared for, loved, and welcomed. First Peter 4:9–10 in the *Living Bible* states it like this:

Cheerfully share your home with those who need a meal or a place to stay for the night. God has given each of you some special abilities; be sure to use them to help each other, passing on to others' God's many kinds of blessings.[14]

These people are those who made you feel welcome when starting a new job, greeted you when visiting a new church, or even someone who invited you to lunch or something. They make strangers feel welcome when everyone else ignores them. An example of someone extending hospitality can be found in the following:

And when she was baptized, and her household, she besought us, saying, if ye have judged me to be faithful to the Lord, come into my house, and abide there. And she constrained us. (Acts 16:15 KJV)

For a bishop must be blameless, as the steward of God, not selfwilled, not soon angry, not given to wine, no striker, not given to filthy lucre: But a lover of hospitality, a lover of good men, sober, just, holy, temperate. (Titus 1:7–8 KJV)

---

[14] *The Living Bible Paraphrased, Special Crusade Edition for the Billy Graham, Evangelistic Association* (Minneapolis: Billy Graham Evangelistic Association, 1972), p. 993.

Knowledge: 1 Corinthians 12:28; Acts 10:9–19; 5:1–4 KJV. The gift of knowledge enables a believer to discover, accumulate, analyze, and clarify information pertinent to the growth and well-being of the body. The believer devotes much of the time reading scriptures and helping others increase their understanding of God's Word. Knowledge is transmitted to you by the Holy Spirit about something or someone that you have no ability or means to know about with your own limited intelligence and knowledge level.

So what does all that mean, and how can this knowledge be applied to our everyday lives? Say you misplaced your keys. You searched everywhere for them and could not find them. Then suddenly, a thought—a word of knowledge, if you will—given to you by the Holy Spirit tells you where your keys were, and you found them exactly where the Holy Spirit said they were. Or maybe a crisis arises, and no one knows how to handle the situation, and you solve the crisis. Or even maybe you get knowledge about what a certain scripture means and how it applies to you. God will give you knowledge about how to witness to individuals on their levels. Maybe even on how to start a business or put on a program in church.

An example about the word of knowledge can be found in the following:

> But a certain man name Ananias, with Sapphira and his wife, sold a possession, and kept back part of the price, his wife also being

privy to it, and brought a certain part, and laid it at the apostles feet. But Peter said, Ananias, why hath Satan filled thine heart to lie to the Holy Ghost, and to keep back part of the land? (Acts 5:1–3 KJV)

And the king of Israel sent to the place which the man of God told him and warned him of, and saved himself there not once nor twice. Therefore the heart of the king of Syria was sore troubled for this thing; and he called his servants, and said unto them, Will ye not show me which of us is for the king of Israel? And one of his servants said, none, my lord, O king; but Elisha, the prophet that is in Israel, telleth the king of Israel the words that thou speaketh in thy bedchamber. (2 Kings 6:10–12 KJV)

Leadership: Acts 7:10–11; Hebrews 13:7; 1 Timothy 5:17 KJV. Leadership, the gift that gives a believer the confidence to step forward, give direction, and provide motivation to fulfill a dream or complete a task. We find this spoken about in Romans 12:8 and 1 Corinthians 12:28 KJV. The more skillful and effective the leadership, the more effective the church or organization runs, and the potential for growth increases. In the church setting, leadership should be appointed by the Lord, and they should follow the leading of the Lord to accomplish their goals. Individuals in leadership positions must remember that the Lord Jesus is the head of the church, and they are just the under-shepherds, carrying out and tending to the needs of the individuals who have been placed in and under their care.

Examples of leadership include:

> One that ruleth well his own house, having his children in subjection with all gravity; (for if a man know not how to rule his own house, how shall he take care of the church of God?). (1 Timothy 3:4–5 KJV)

> Obey them that have the rule over you, and submit yourselves: for they watch for your souls, as they that must give account, that they may do it with joy, and not with grief: for that is unprofitable for you. (Hebrews 13:17 KJV)

Mercy: Romans 12:8; Acts 16:33–34; Mark 9:41; Acts 11:28–30; Luke 10:33–35; Matthew 25:34–40 KJV. Mercy is the gift or ability to feel genuine empathy and compassion for individuals who suffer distresses, whether they are physical, emotional, or mental. And they can grieve with those who grieve. People with this gift are sensitive to the feelings and circumstances of others and can quickly discern when someone is not doing well. We often say, "God's grace and mercy be toward us." An excellent example of someone showing mercy is the story of the good Samaritan in Luke 10:30–37 (KJV).

If not for God's mercy and the discernment of the Spirit, we would see many more suicides. But because of God's mercy, he sends someone with this gift to show people God's love and that he cares for them. Matthew 5:7 (KJV) states, "Blessed are the merciful for they shall obtain mercy."

So to sum up mercy, it is what we express when we are led by God to be compassionate in our words, attitudes, and actions. Again, an example of mercy can be found in Luke 10:30–37 (KJV), the parable of the good Samaritan which I will quote in part:

> But a certain Samaritan, as he journeyed, came where he was: and when he saw him, he had compassion on him, and went to him, and bound up his wounds, pouring in oil and wine, and set him on his own beast, and brought him to an inn, and took care of him. (Luke 10:33–34 KJV)

And in Romans 12:8 (KJV),

> Or he that exhorteth, on exhortation: he that giveth, let him do it with simplicity; he that ruleth, with diligence; he that sheweth mercy, with cheerfulness.

Preaching: 2 Timothy 1:16–18; Romans 12:7; Acts 6:1–7; Titus 3:14; Galatians 6:2,10 KJV. Preaching is the supernatural ability to communicate effectively and proclaim the Word of God, providing insight, warning, correction, and encouragement as given to them by the inspiration of the Holy Spirit. Something like a shepherd who cares for the sheep that are assigned to them, through caring for their spiritual needs, teaching them the truth, and praying for the sick. Pastors are first and foremost servants, as are all the children of God who have been endowed with spiritual gifts. The main purpose or goal of a pastor is to reveal Christ to the people through teaching and preaching the Word of God.

> Preach the word, be instant in season, out of season; reprove, rebuke, exhort with all long-suffering and doctrine. For the time will come when they will not endure sound doctrine; but after their own lusts shall they heap to themselves teachers, having itching ears; and they shall turn away their ears from the truth, and shall be turned unto fables. (2 Timothy 4:2–4 KJV)

> For Christ sent me not to baptize, but to preach the gospel: not with wisdom of words, lest the cross of Christ should be made of none effect. For the preaching of the cross

is to them that perish foolishness; but unto us which are saved it is the power of God. (1 Corinthians 1: 17–18 KJV)

Service: Romans 12:6–7 KJV. The gift of services means to invest the talents one has in the life and ministry of other members of the body and the ability to meet the needs of others in practical ways. A person who serves, or ministers, helps others accomplish spiritual goals by freeing them from routine but necessary duties. Here is an example of service:

> Then the twelve called the multitude of the disciples unto them, and said, it is not reason that we should leave the word of God, and serve tables. Wherefore, brethren, look ye out among you seven men of honest report, full of the Holy Ghost and wisdom, whom we may appoint over this business. (Acts 6:2–3 KJV)

Pastoring: 1 Timothy 3:1–7; John 10:1–18; 1 Peter 5:1–3 KJV. Pastoring is the gift that gives a believer the ability, confidence, capability, and compassion to provide spiritual leadership and direction for individuals or groups of believers. Examples of pastoring in the Bible include the following:

> Take heed therefore unto yourselves, and to all the flock, over the which the Holy Ghost

hath made you overseers, to feed the church of God, which he hath purchased with his own blood. (Acts 20:28 KJV)

But the word of the Lord endureth for ever. And this is the word by which the gospel is preached unto you. (1 Peter 1:25 KJV)

Teaching: Romans 12:6–7; 1 Corinthians 12:28; 2 Timothy 2:15; Acts 13:1; 18:24–28 KJV. The gift that enables a believer to communicate a personal understanding of the Bible and faith in such a way that it becomes clear and understood by others. Here again the role of the pastor-teacher comes into effect. It is this gift that enables you to discern between what is biblical and what is secular. The Christian teacher is necessary even more today because of the various cults that have woven themselves into society, each teaching a different doctrine than what the Bible teaches.

The Christian teacher must be filled with the Holy Spirit and understand the Word of God. They must hold to the doctrine that Jesus Christ is Lord and be able to prove it with their teaching. It is important that the Christian teacher adhere to the scripture of 2 Timothy 2:15 (KJV): "Study to shew thyself approved unto God, a workman that needeth not to be ashamed, rightly dividing the word of truth."

In these last days, without a clear understanding of the scriptures, misinterpretation and misunderstanding cause the message of the cross to become lost to this evil and dying world.

> For when the time ye ought to be teachers, ye
> have need that one teach you again which be
> the first principles of the oracles of God; and
> are become such as have need of milk, and not
> of strong drink. (Hebrews 5:12 KJV)

Wisdom: 1 Corinthians 2:1–13; 12:8; Acts 6:3, 10; James 1:5–6; 2 Peter 3:15 KJV. The gift of wisdom allows the believer to sort through opinions, facts, and thoughts to determine what solution would be best for the individual believer or the community. Here again we must rely on the leading of the Holy Spirit to guide us. This guidance comes through daily fellowship with the Holy Spirit and through reading the Word of God. We refer to 1 Corinthians 2:6–8 (KJV), which states:

> Howbeit we speak wisdom among them that
> are perfect: yet not the wisdom of this world,
> nor of the princes of this world, that come to
> nought: but we speak of the wisdom of God
> in a mystery, even the hidden wisdom, which
> God ordained before the world unto our glory.

James 1:5 (KJV) tells us, "If any of you lack wisdom, let him ask of God, that giveth to all men liberally, and upbraideth not; and it shall be given him."

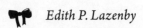

CHAPTER 6
Questions

1. What does evangelism mean?

   _____

   _____

   _____

   _____

2. Does everyone have leadership ability? If yes, why? If not, why not?

   _____

   _____

   _____

   _____

3. What scriptures can you find "giving" in?

   _____

   _____

   _____

   _____

4. What is faith?

   _____

   _____

   _____

   _____

5. What is the difference between preaching and teaching?

_____

_____

_____

_____

6. Name some instances of "helps" in the Old Testament.

_____

_____

_____

_____

7. What three things does exhortation do?

_____

_____

_____

_____

CHAPTER 7

Stir Up Your Spiritual Gift

> Wherefore I put thee in remembrance that
> thou stir up the gift of God, which is in thee
> by the putting on of my hands.
>
> —2 Timothy 1:6 KJV

In this scripture, Paul is admonishing Timothy to stir up the gift that is in him by the putting on of his hands. This is all well and good, but suppose no one has laid his or her hands on you. How do you stir up the gift the Holy Spirit deposited within you?

This will take us, as individuals, acting on what we have read in the scriptures and the anointing of the Holy Spirit to bring back to our rememberance what we have read in the Bible. We must look at the four Gospels as well as the book of Acts to discern what gifts were in operation through Jesus, Peter, Paul, and the other disciples.

Jesus told us in John 14:12 (KJV), "Verily, verily, I say unto you, He that believeth on me, the works that I do shall he do also; and greater works than these shall he do, because I go unto my Father."

But earlier, in Mark 16:15–18 (KJV), Jesus told his disciples which we become once we accept Jesus as our Lord and Savior to,

> Go ye into all the world, and preach the gospel to every creature. He that believeth and is baptized shall be saved, but he that believeth not shall be damned. And these signs shall follow them that believe; In my name shall they cast out devils: they shall speak with new tongues; they shall take up serpents; and if they drink any deadly thing, it shall not hurt them; they shall lay hands on the sick, and they shall recover.

All this is done in faith. You have faith because if you did not, you would not be a child of God. Let me break this down. It took faith to believe that Jesus died for your sins. Through repenting and asking Jesus to forgive you of your sins, and to come into your life to be your Lord and Savior, you asked an unseen entity to do this for you believing this to be fact, which it is.

We read in James 2:17–18 (KJV), "Even so faith, if it hath not works, is dead, being alone. Yea, a man may say, thou hast faith, and I have works: shew me thy faith without thy works, and I will shew thee my faith by my works."

So we need to step out and exercise our faith when directed to do so by the Lord. So how do you know the Lord is speaking to you? God speaks to you through dreams, visions, impressions, his Word, a still small voice, and a willingness to obey and yield to the prompting of the Holy Spirit. God is not going to ask you to do anything contrary to his will and the Word of God.

According to scripture there are many gifts in the body of Christ. But unfortunately, a lot of these gifts are lying dormant, waiting to be activated. The list of gifts I have provided is not exhaustive because God can and will give gifts to whoever he desires to give a gift. I believe the apostle Paul listed these gifts as examples of how God uses the Holy Spirit to give gifts to believers. It could be a gift not listed here but chosen by God to empower an individual. Some people say there are only a finite number of gifts. But in actuality, we cannot put a limit on God and the gifts he has for us.

So the question is how does a person activate the gift you have been given by the Holy Spirit? The most common answer is by practice. Let me ask you a question.

Since you've been saved, is there a particular area that you find yourself wanting more information about, such as knowing something about a person you never knew before? Perhaps knowing someone has a headache or some other ailment, or maybe all of a sudden you have compassion for someone when in the past you did not. Maybe you are around a person and suddenly experience a headache. Or maybe your leg starts hurting, and you know there is no reason for you to be experiencing these things. So the door of opportunity is opened for you to ask the individual, "Do you have a headache?" Or, "Does your leg hurt?"

If they apply in the affirmative, then you know God has given you a word of knowledge about that individual. Now you need to pray for the person because most likely, God has given you the ability to lay hands on people and pray that they be healed in Jesus's name. I say Jesus's name because there is no other name that can be used to glorify God in heaven. And all we do we do in Jesus's name.

One thing should be mentioned here. For a person to operate effectively in the gifts of the Spirit, you must know the Word of God. And it is essential that you have an active prayer life. We must stay in contact with the One who is giving us the gift, or gifts, so we will not become puffed up and think we are performing the miracles that might be occurring. We need to stay in prayer so we will know when God speaks to us.

We must become attuned to God's voice and not our thoughts or the thoughts of the enemy. Whatever we do when using the gift God has given us, we want to bring glory to him. So it is a must that we study the Word, memorize the Word, and allow the Word to become a part of you. The Word states in part in 2 Timothy 2:15 (KJV), "study to show thyself approved unto God." And in Psalm 119:11 (KJV), "thy word have I hid in mine heart, that I might not sin against thee."

In Joshua 1:8 (KJV), we read, "this book of the law shall not depart out of thy mouth; but thou shall mediate therein day and night, that thou mayest observe to do according to all that is written therein." Paul exhorted Timothy in 2 Timothy 1:6 (KJV), "Therefore I remind you to stir up the gift of God which is in you though the laying on of my hands." First Peter 4:10 (KJV) tells us, "As every man hath received the gift, even so minister the same to another, as good stewards of the manifold grace of God."

Sometimes you need to stir up the gift with which you have been endowed. You possibly may need to find someone who moves in your gift to mentor you so you will know how to move or operate in your gift. So how do you stir up a gift you do not know you have, and no one has laid his or her hands on you or prayed for you?

When you were born again, the day you accepted Jesus Christ into your life as your Lord and Savior, you received the Holy Spirit into your spirit man, which was dead, but is now alive in Jesus. Since you now have the Holy Spirit living inside you, you can do all things through Christ, through faith, just as Jesus did when he was here in his human form. Jesus said in Mark 16:16–18 (KJV),

> He that believeth and is baptized shall be saved; but he that believeth not shall be damned. And these signs shall follow them that believe; In my name shall they cast out devils; they shall speak with new tongues:

They shall take up serpents; and if they drink any deadly thing, it shall not hurt them; and they shall lay hands on the sick and they shall recover.

These gifts have already been placed in you. It's left to you to step out in faith and exercise the feeling you have experienced. Maybe you heard in your inner man to pray for someone, or maybe a thought came to you about someone with whom you were talking. This is your opportunity to ask a question about something you feel—maybe a pain somewhere. Maybe you saw someone's foot in a cast and had an urge to pray for the individual, with permission, for the foot to be healed.

Yes, the examples provided in this chapter were meant to give you the opportunity to step out in faith and exercise the gift within you. Stir up that gift. Start using or speaking in whatever gift you feel you have started to operate in. Your gift could be praying for someone, speaking in tongues, or even giving a word of comfort to someone. You must practice your gift to perfect your gift even though it is given to you by God.

Not only must we read the Word of God and pray, we must fast because fasting crucifies the flesh and helps to eliminate bad habits from our lives. Fasting also helps you to have dominion over your flesh, and you become more sensitive to the voice of God. Jesus told us in his Word certain things only come through fasting and prayer. We must learn how to crucify the flesh if we want to be used by God. We need to spend time reading and meditating on the Word of God because as you use the gift you have been given, you will notice that it is never contrary to God's Word.

Let us look at fasting for a moment. What does fasting accomplish? For one thing, fasting can help to break bad habits. It can produce a new heart and closeness to God. David, in the book of Psalms, states, "create in me a clean heart, O God, and renew a right spirit within me" (Psalm 51:10 KJV). The only way we can get clean or new hearts within us is dying to self and yielding to the Spirit.

How you fast can be determined by God or you. Do not be like the Pharisees. When they fasted, they wanted everyone to see them. In other words, "Look at what I am doing. I am fasting. I'm crucifying my flesh. I'm giving up the pleasure of eating." No, that is not what we want to do. Remember what you do in secret you will be rewarded for openly by God.

If you check the scriptures, you will see that everywhere Jesus went, signs and wonders followed him. On the day of Pentecost, fifty days after Jesus's ascension into heaven, he sent back the Holy Spirit known as the Comforter to empower us. So why are we so afraid to step out and use the gift that is lying dormant within us? It's because we haven't been told that there is a gift in us given to us the moment we accept Jesus.

Since we do not know this information, we cannot in

good faith act on what we don't know. But thanks be to God, who gives us the victory. Once we learn we have a gift, we can act on that information and begin to stir ourselves up and find out what we have. We have been so brainwashed that we believe only leaders are endowed with gifts from God. This is not true. It's time to learn what gift you have been endowed with and start moving in the power of the Holy Spirit.

As of today—this moment—we as individuals can turn things around and receive what God has for us. We need to become inquisitive and find out if we are missing something when we go to church or fellowship with other believers. We need to get out of our comfort zones and do what God has called us to do because we are truly without any excuse for failing to seek God and see what his Word means when it states he gave gifts to men. What gifts? Do I have a gift, and if so, what is it? We just cannot sit by and wait for others to act on our behalf.

By discovering your spiritual gift, you can clarify God's will for your life. And by using that gift, you will bring glory to God. And these signs shall follow those who believe. Whatever your gift might be, God will never call you to a position without first giving you the gifts you need to be successful in your position. When you know what your spiritual gift is, that will help you to make wise decisions. First Corinthians chapter 12 tells us how each part of the human body helps to make up the whole body. The gifts of God help make up the full body of Christ. Since Christ cannot be here physically, even though he is the head of the church, he uses us to build up the body of the church. We are the joints, ligaments, bones, and muscles, and through us, the church grows because we are edifying Christ.

There would be no more competition, no more jealousy, no more complaining, no more paralyzed body parts because we would grow in numbers, we would grow in grace, and we would grow in love for each other. We find these words in 1 Peter 4:10–11 (KJV):

> As every man hath received the gift, even so minister the same one to another, as good stewards of the manifold grace of God. If any man speak, let him speak as the oracles of God, if any man minister, let him do it as of the ability which God giveth; that God in all things may be glorified through Jesus Christ, to whom be praise and dominion forever and ever. Amen.

The Living Bible states it this way:

> God has given each of you some special abilities; be sure to use them to help each other, passing on to others God's many kinds of blessings. Are you called to preach? Then preach as though God himself were speaking through you. Are you called to help others? Do it with all the strength and energy that

God supplies, so that God will be glorified through Jesus Christ—to him be glory and power forever and ever. Amen.[15]

Only God gets the glory using the gifts he has placed in you as you step out in faith and use them.

We as individuals need to do what Paul admonished Timothy to do, and that is to stir up the gift that is within you because you have a word for someone. Someone is waiting for you to pray for him or her. Someone is waiting for you to lay hands on him or her to be healed through the power of the Holy Spirit. People are waiting for you to prophesy to them to verify what God has told them. And on and on.

It is imperative that we learn to recognize and flow in the gifts of the Holy Spirit. It is not only a blessing to us; the lives of other people may depend on it. You are carrying someone's miracle. Do not let it stay inside you. It is time to use what God has given you to help someone else in the body of Christ. Stir it up. Stir that gift up, and use it to the glory of God.

As I conclude, if you have received the gift of speaking in other tongues, it's time to use this gift and pray in tongues often. This gift is for everyone as described in Acts 2:38–39 (KJV):

---

[15] *The Living Bible*, p. 993.

Then Peter said unto them, Repent, and be baptized every one of you in the name of Jesus Christ for the remission of sins, and ye shall receive the gift of the Holy Ghost. For the promise is unto you, and to your children, and to all that are afar off, even as many as the Lord our God shall call.

Ask the Lord to fill you with his Spirit with the evidence of speaking in other tongues, and then pray often in your prayer language. Start at about fifteen minutes and then for as long as the Spirit leads you to speak in tongues. Or praise God with worship music to stir up the gift. If you are getting ready to pray for someone who is sick or needs prayer, ask the Lord to stir up the gift that is within you so he may get the glory. Then ask the person if he or she will receive his healing. If not sure, do not minister healing. Give the person healing scriptures to build his or her faith, such as Jeremiah 30:17; Psalm 103:1–4; Isaiah 53:4; Galatians 3:13; and Mark 16:18 KJV.

The more you worship God in prayer or pray in tongues, the more the Spirit helps your human spirit to be more sensitive to him. Then whenever he wants to operate in any of these spiritual gifts, he is able to manifest his abilities effectively through believers, especially if the believers are open or yielding to his leading or unction.

Do not let anyone discourage you and tell you the gifts of God are not for today, they died with the apostles, or some other excuse to keep you from seeking the Lord and enjoying all the benefits he has for you. If the gifts died with the apostles, they would have been left out of the Bible, and we would not know about them. But they are there. Now stir up what is inside you.

CHAPTER 7
Questions

1. How do you stir up your gift?

_____

_____

_____

_____

2. Quote James 2:17–18 KJV.

_____

_____

_____

_____

3. Are the gifts of God limited or unlimited? Why?

_____

_____

_____

_____

4. What is the purpose of fasting?

_____

_____

_____

_____

5. Have you discovered your spiritual gift, and are you using it (them)?

_____

_____

_____

_____

6. Are spiritual gifts for everyone? Explain.

_____

_____

_____

_____

7. What are the gifts used for?

_____

_____

_____

_____

8. Quote 1 Peter 4:10 KJV.

_____

_____

_____

_____

CHAPTER 8

Prayer and Intercession

Two gifts in the body of Christ are not mentioned in the lists of spiritual gifts though they are very important. These gifts are prayer and intercession. Everyone should know how to pray. I said, "should," because not everyone knows how to pray. First of all, let us define prayer. Prayer is two-way communication between God and humankind. It's like going to your parents and friends, talking with them, and telling them about problems you may have.

As I stated above, prayer is talking with God. You don't have to be a preacher, bishop, or even have a title to pray or to be used by God. The most important thing is that you are a willing vessel to be used by the Lord. Throughout the Bible you will find that practically nothing was accomplished without prayer. Take Abraham, for instance. He lived among people who worshipped idols, but Abraham somehow knew that God was not an idol. Abraham looked at the heavens, just as we are able to look at the heavens, and saw that the handiwork was not made by humans.

Genesis 1:1 (KJV) states, "In the beginning God created the heaven and the earth." It was God. The Word of God also tells us that if we search for God with all our hearts, we will find him. In Hebrews 11:6 (KJV) we find, "But without faith it is impossible to please him; for he that cometh to God must believe that he is, and that he is a rewarder of them that diligently seek him."

Abraham exercised two things he did not even know existed: the gift of faith, and one of the fruit of the spirit, faith. It took faith to believe there must be someone or something that existed besides idols, which he had probably seen and heard people worshipping. It was likely that Abraham assumed there was someone higher than he was, and he probably prayed to this entity believing he would answer. And one day God spoke to him. His prayers were answered, and from that time his heart yearned to follow this God person who spoke to his heart.

Moses escaped being killed by the Pharaoh of his time because the Jewish people were increasing in number and had started to outnumber the Egyptians (Exodus 1:9 KJV). The Pharaoh wanted all newborn Jewish boys slain to quench the spread of the men of Israel. But God had a plan for Moses's life, just as God has a plan for your life. That is why he has endowed you with gifts. But the enemy does not want you to know what is inside you. Even though Moses was raised by Pharaoh's daughter, God also used his mother and sister to instill in him his Jewish roots. God gave Moses the wisdom and know-how to lead a million

Jewish inhabitants out of Egypt into the Promised Land. But the Israelites, because of their hearts' hardness and unbelief, caused themselves to wander in the wilderness for forty years.

Elisha had the gift of discerning of spirits, but he did not know this was a gift because he relied on God for protection. Elisha was doing what God called him to do. Elisha saw in the spiritual realm whereas his servant saw in the natural. According to 2 Kings 6:17 (KJV), the Syrian army came to Dothan to capture Elisha. When Elisha's servant woke up that morning and saw the city was surrounded by the Syrian army, he was terrified. But Elisha told him not to worry because there were more with them than with the Syrians. Here, prophecy is seen in action because he foretold what he saw in the Spirit. He comforted the young man with those words, especially when his eyes were opened. The gift of discerning spirits, faith, and the word of knowledge were in operation through Elisha.

Jeremiah, a prophet of the Lord from birth, came to a point in his life when he did not want to prophecy anymore because he spoke the truth, but the people did not want to hear the truth. This resulted in Jeremiah being kept in awful situations to survive.

When the tribes of Moab, Amman, and Mount Seir came against Judah and Jerusalem, King Jehoshaphat sought the Lord through fasting and prayer as to what he and his people should do. The Lord let Jehoshaphat know through the prophet Jahaziel that the battle was not his, but God's (2 Chronicles 20:15 KJV). God even gave the king instructions on how the battle would be fought (2 Chronicles 20:16–17 KJV). God answers prayers.

Esther was a young Jewish woman chosen by the king to be his wife after he exiled his first wife, Vasthi, for disobedience and failure to follow instructions. When Esther found out that the evil man Haman had sent a decree throughout the land that on a particular day the Jewish people would be annihilated, she called a three-day fast and prayed, seeking the direction from God about what to do.

Joel prophesied a word of knowledge. The gift of prophecy and the word of knowledge were in operation when God gave him knowledge of what was and what is to come in the last days.

But you say all that happened in the Old Testament. Yes, that is true. But in the New Testament, we see Jesus did not start his ministry until he was baptized. Then he went into the wilderness, where he fasted and prayed forty days and forty nights.

So how does intercession fit in as a gift? God has someone praying for situations to be reversed. An example of this can be found in Genesis, when Joseph's brothers wanted to kill him because of jealousy. But one brother, Rueben, interceded and said not to slay him (Geneses 37:20–21 KJV). And Joseph wound up being sold into slavery.

Moses interceded for the children of Israel when God wanted to destroy them for their heart hardness (Exodus

32:1–14 KJV). Prayers of the intercessors kept back the enemy's evil intents. It's Satan plan to destroy humankind and take as many as he can to spend eternity with him in hell.

The disciples saw how important prayer was and asked Jesus to teach them to pray. Jesus gave them a model to follow, which can be found in Matthew 6:9–18 and Luke 11:2–4 KJV. Peter went to a house to pray one day, and while he was praying, a sheet came down from heaven. God was able to let Peter know through this vision what he had called clean Peter was not to call unclean (Acts 10:9–16 KJV).

Prayer is such a necessity that, as I mentioned previously, before Jesus started his ministry, he was baptized, and then the Spirit led him into the wilderness, where he fasted and prayed for forty days and forty nights (Matthew 4:1–2 KJV). After forty days and forty nights, the devil tempted Jesus.

Prayer is necessary before any gift is put into operation because we want to make sure we are hearing from the Lord and doing what he is instructing us to do, not following our fleshly desires. This is why it is important that we seek God to find out what gift or gifts he has given us. And you should not be jealous because you do not have a gift someone else has. Remember, one gift is not better than another.

Even as Jesus was tempted by the devil, once you start living for Jesus, the devil will tempt you. This goes for any gift you may have been blessed with; even if you pray for someone, you will be tempted or discouraged by the adversary. Don't take prayer lightly because there is power in prayer. Prayer may mean a matter of life or death to someone when you get an unction to pray for an individual or an event or whatever God wants you to pray for.

Let me give you a testimony of what happened to me. Some things you just cannot forget. They stay fresh in your mind to remind you of the greatness of God. When I was younger, working, and living with my parents, one day I had to work the evening shift. My parents decided to take a trip to Washington, DC, to visit my mother's sister, who was ailing. It was early in the morning. I kissed them goodbye and told them to be safe and to say hello to everyone for me. I saw them off and went back to bed.

The Lord woke me up, and I heard in my spirit, *Pray, danger.* I had no idea what was going on, but I assumed my parents were in trouble. I started to pray in the natural and then in tongues. I didn't know what was wrong, but you know, sometimes you just know that you know something, but you cannot explain it. When the heaviness left, I felt in my spirit everything was okay.

Later that morning, my mother called me and told me what happened to them. As they came out of the Holland Tunnel, the car blew a tire and began to swerve all over the road. Dad was able to bring the car under control, and a policeman who was there saw what was happening and went to help my parents. Thank God I was obedient because anything could have happened. The outcome could have been much different had I not obeyed and prayed.

Even though I did not know at the time, gifts were in operation. The gift of knowing, the gift of faith, and discerning of Spirit. I was awakened and discerned something was wrong. And knowing that it was the Lord who woke me up, I had to pray. Have you ever woken up with the feeling something was wrong and started praying for an individual or something that was about to take place? Listen to your inner man, and you will not be sorry.

Another incident that happened to me occurred one evening as I was praying in English and tongues. A heaviness came over me. I started praying and rebuking the spirit of death. I was in a spiritual battle for someone named Eloise, and this lasted for approximately fifteen to twenty minutes. I had no idea why this was happening or the urgency, but I knew I had to be obedient to what I was feeling. I did not find out until approximately one week later what happened and why I was rebuking the spirit of death for one named Eloise.

Our friend named Eloise lived in North Carolina, and she was in the hospital. This is what she related to my mother, who then related this to me because I had shared my experience with my mother. Eloise told my mother she was in the hospital, and the death angel came into her room to take her. But she pleaded with the Lord not to take her yet because she had some unfinished business to attend to. She told my mother the death angel went into the room next door and took the lady in that bed. Eloise lived approximately six months longer. I assume she was able to take care of whatever she had to take care of. Had I not interceded for Eloise, I believe that night Eloise would have departed this life.

What am I saying? Prayer and intercession go hand in hand. Even though you are not in the limelight, and everyone does not see what you are doing, you are doing what God has called you to do. The Lord gets the glory because your prayers stop the hand of the enemy. When you feel the urgency to pray for someone, maybe you know that person and maybe you do not. Just follow the Lord's lead. His or her life may depend on your prayers. We are in a spiritual battle, and obedience is the key. The gifts have been given to us to use. The enemy does not want you to know what is inside you; it is his job to keep you ignorant. It's our job to enlighten you about what God has given you to defeat the enemy. And it is our job to expose the enemy in whatever capacity the Lord uses us in. Let us pray:

> Father, in the precious name of Jesus, I thank you for the gifts that are within us. We have sat on them long enough, not knowing that we were holding these precious gems inside us. Since I have read this book, my heart yearns to stir up the gift that is within me to be used for your glory and to help those you direct

me to, where they will be healed, comforted, or just hear an encouraging word from you through prophecy or whatever gift you gifted me with. Thank you Jesus. Amen.

BIBLIOGRAPHY

Hagin, Kenneth E. *The Holy Spirit and His Gifts Study Course*. Tulsa, OK: Faith Library Publication, 1991.

The Holy Spirit. Grand Rapids, MI: Academic Books, Zondervan Publishing House, 1958.

The Living Bible Paraphrased, Special Crusade Edition for the Billy Graham Evangelistic Association. Minneapolis: Billy Graham Evangelistic Association, 1972.

Merriam-Webster.com/dictionary/supernatural.

The Scofield Study Bible. Oxford: Oxford University Press, 1996.

Unger, Merrill F. *Unger's Bible Dictionary*. Chicago: Moody Press, 1987.

Webster's New World Dictionary of the American Language: College Edition. Cleveland and New York: The World Publishing Company, 1966.